Building Reusable Rockets

Gregory Vogt

D1210905

AV² provides enriched content that supplements and complements this book. Weigl's AV² books strive to create inspired learning and engage young minds in a total learning experience.

Your AV² Media Enhanced books come alive with...

Audio
Listen to sections of the book read aloud.

Key Words
Study vocabulary, and complete a matching word activity.

Video
Watch informative video clips.

Quizzes
Test your knowledge.

Embedded Weblinks
Gain additional information for research.

Slideshow
View images and captions, and prepare a presentation.

Try This!
Complete activities and hands-on experiments.

... and much, much more!

Go to **www.av2books.com,** and enter this book's unique code.

BOOK CODE

A V H 9 2 3 8 3

AV² by Weigl brings you media enhanced books that support active learning.

Published by AV² by Weigl
350 5ᵗʰ Avenue, 59ᵗʰ Floor
New York, NY 10118
Website: www.av2books.com

Library of Congress Cataloging-in-Publication Data

Names: Vogt, Gregory, author.
Title: Building reusable rockets / Gregory L. Vogt.
Description: New York, NY : AV2 by Weigl, [2019] | Series: Space exploration | Audience: Grade 7 to 8. | Includes index.
Identifiers: LCCN 2018053512 (print) | LCCN 2018054168 (ebook) | ISBN 9781489698285 (Multi User ebook) | ISBN 9781489698292 (Single User ebook) | ISBN 9781489698261 (hardcover : alk. paper) | ISBN 9781489698278 (softcover : alk. paper)
Subjects: LCSH: Rockets (Aeronautics)--Juvenile literature. | Reusable space vehicles--Juvenile literature.
Classification: LCC TL782.5 (ebook) | LCC TL782.5 .V588 2019 (print) | DDC 629.47/5--dc23
LC record available at https://lccn.loc.gov/2018053512

Printed in Guangzhou, China
1 2 3 4 5 6 7 8 9 0 23 22 21 20 19

032019
112318

Project Coordinator: Heather Kissock   Designer: Ana María Vidal

Every reasonable effort has been made to trace ownership and to obtain permission to reprint copyright material. The publishers would be pleased to have any errors or omissions brought to their attention so that they may be corrected in subsequent printings.

Weigl acknowledges Alamy, Getty Images, iStock, Newscom, and Shutterstock as its primary image suppliers for this title.

First published by North Star Editions in 2018.

CONTENTS

Chapter 1

Blasting Off

Imagine boarding a **capsule** at the top of a tall rocket. You and five other space tourists strap yourselves in to a reclined seat that faces upward. The countdown reaches zero, and the rocket engines fire, launching the spacecraft. A few minutes after liftoff, the capsule separates from the rocket. As the rocket heads back to the launch site, the capsule coasts upward. Large windows give spectacular views of the blue curve of Earth.

Someday, reusable rockets may allow space tourists to orbit Earth.

Then, the capsule begins falling back to Earth. It plows into the **atmosphere**. Next, its parachutes open. Just above the ground, thruster rockets slow the capsule for a soft landing. You leave the capsule, and it is prepared for the next flight. The capsule is mounted on top of a rocket again. This rocket is refueled. Soon, the next group of space tourists will board.

People have used rockets for hundreds of years. Chinese fireworks began using rockets in the 1200s CE. Large arrows were attached to tubes filled with gunpowder. When the rocket was ignited, the arrow flew a long distance.

In **1232 BC**, the **Chinese** used **rocket-arrows** in their **war** with the **Mongols**.

In the 1950s, scientists and engineers worked to launch **satellites** into space. One of these scientists was Wernher von Braun. Von Braun was the main designer of the Saturn V rocket. This rocket launched astronauts to the Moon.

The **Saturn V** rocket carried **318,000** gallons (1.2 million liters) of **liquid oxygen**.

However, the Saturn V rocket could be used only one time. Von Braun wanted to build rockets that could travel to and from space many times.

From 1960–1972, the Saturn V rockets were the backbone of the U.S. space program. They carried astronauts to the Moon.

Von Braun designed a giant rocket with a winged spacecraft on top. His design had three main parts called **stages**. The stages would stack on top of one another. The first stage would be a huge rocket with 51 engines. When this rocket ran out of fuel, it would fall back to Earth. Parachutes would bring it back safely so it could be used again.

After the rocket's first stage detached, the second stage would ignite. This stage would also parachute back and be reused. The third stage would be a winged spacecraft. It would **orbit** Earth before flying home to a runway.

However, Von Braun's reusable rocket was never built. It was too complicated and expensive. At the time, engineers were only beginning to learn how to build space rockets. Many rockets crashed or exploded right after liftoff. Each failure meant going back to the drawing board to try again.

Reusable rockets took years of hard work to develop. However, new materials and technologies have become available. A few private companies have begun to build and launch reusable rockets.

Elon Musk founded the company SpaceX, which creates reusable rockets.

Chapter 2

It's Rocket Science

Rocket science is all about thrust. Thrust is a pushing force that propels the rocket forward. **Propellants** are pumped to the rocket's engines, where they are burned. This process creates hot gases. These gases are channeled so they are released in just one direction. When the gases leave the rocket's engine, thrust is created. When enough thrust is produced, the rocket lifts off the ground.

Blue Origin's New Shepard rocket is designed for a vertical landing.

As the gas shoots out of the engine, the rocket moves in the opposite direction. Engines that shoot out more gas will produce more thrust. More thrust makes the rocket move faster. Increasing the gas's speed will also produce more thrust.

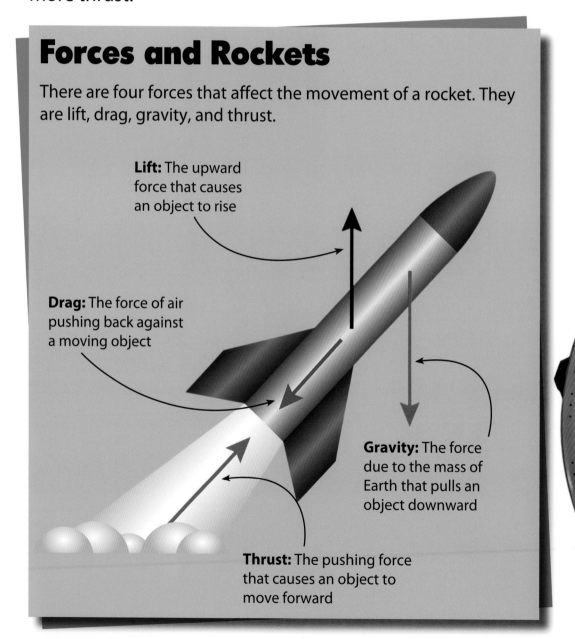

Forces and Rockets

There are four forces that affect the movement of a rocket. They are lift, drag, gravity, and thrust.

Lift: The upward force that causes an object to rise

Drag: The force of air pushing back against a moving object

Gravity: The force due to the mass of Earth that pulls an object downward

Thrust: The pushing force that causes an object to move forward

Engineers try to design a rocket's body to be as light as possible. That's because heavier rockets require more force to move. To produce more force, rockets need more propellants. However, some propellants, such as hydrogen and oxygen, must be kept in separate tanks. That makes the rocket heavier. Burning propellants also creates a lot of heat, so engines need a cooling system.

Huge tanks are constructed to hold propellant for rockets.

Rockets also need a steering system. A simple steering system uses fins. These small wings stick out from the rocket's side. The fins act like the feathers on an arrow that keep it flying straight. If the rocket goes off course, the fins can tilt. Air will hit the tilted fins and push the rocket back to the right path. Other steering systems use engines that tilt. If the rocket goes off course, the engines tilt the other way. Then they fire gas to push the rocket back on course.

Rockets may have a **payload** carrier as well. Payloads can be anything from satellites that orbit Earth to spacecraft that travel to other planets. A shell called a fairing covers the payload for launch. Once the rocket is in space, the shell opens to release the payload.

THINK ABOUT IT

A reusable rocket must be able to take off and land. Why would making a rocket reusable double the engineering challenges?

Landing a rocket is difficult. For instance, suppose a rocket is flying back to a landing zone. First, the rocket's engines must restart to slow the rocket's fall. Just above the ground, the speed must reach zero, or else the rocket will crash. Then, landing feet must extend as the rocket touches down.

The Orbital CRS ATK will begin carrying cargo to the International Space Station in 2019.

Space shuttles carried crew members and supplies to the International Space Station.

Chapter 3

Trial and Error

The first partially reusable rocket was actually a space shuttle. The National Aeronautics and Space Administration (NASA) flew the first shuttle in 1981. The shuttle was made up of four parts. A winged spaceship called an orbiter carried astronauts and payloads. The orbiter attached to the side of a huge propellant tank. Two **booster** rockets also attached to the tank.

During liftoff, the boosters quickly used up their fuel. Then they fell from the shuttle and parachuted into the ocean. They floated until ships found them and towed them back to land to be reused.

Minutes later, the propellant tank also dropped off the rocket. Unlike the boosters, it would not be used again. Instead, **friction** with the air caused the tank to burn up as it fell back toward Earth.

Next, the orbiter used small engines on its tail to rocket into orbit. When the shuttle's mission was over, astronauts flew the orbiter back to Earth. There, it landed on a runway. Then the orbiter could be reused for more space missions.

Making parts of the shuttle reusable was supposed to save money on space launches. However, the space shuttle was too complicated to make quick and cheap flights possible.

The rocket booster from the space shuttle *Discovery* landed in the Atlantic Ocean on December 10, 2006.

In 1996, NASA tried to develop a fully reusable rocket. It was called X-33. The X-33 was designed to be launched upright. No parts would fall off on the way to outer space. Instead, the entire rocket would return from space and land on a runway. Tail fins and small wings would allow the X-33 to fly like an airplane on its return.

NASA engineers began testing this design. However, they had problems creating the propellant tanks. The tanks needed to hold massive amounts of propellant. However, they also needed to be very light. Engineers could not figure out how to make the tanks do this. Plans for the X-33 rocket were canceled a few years later, in 2001.

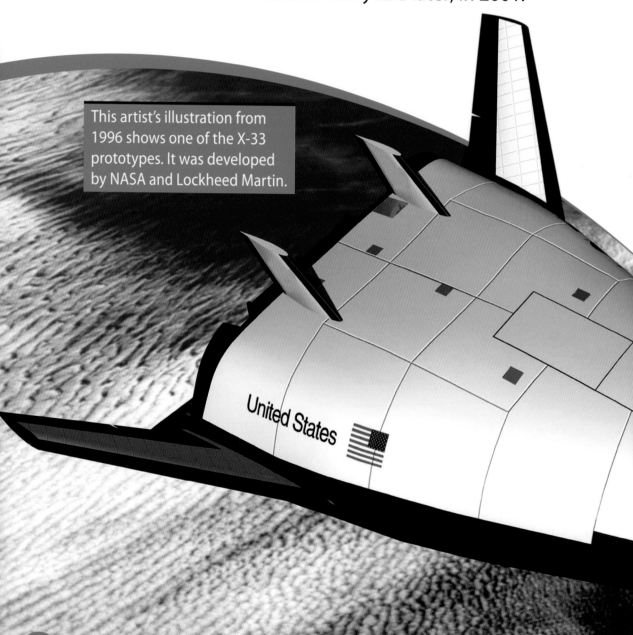

This artist's illustration from 1996 shows one of the X-33 prototypes. It was developed by NASA and Lockheed Martin.

In 2004, President George W. Bush announced that NASA would phase out the space shuttle program in a few years. NASA would keep using the space shuttles to finish building the International Space Station (ISS). However, after that, NASA would focus on missions to deep space. Canceling the space shuttles would allow NASA to devote more time and money to this goal.

However, canceling the shuttles would create a problem. U.S. astronauts would still need a way to travel to and from the ISS. By the time the ISS was completed in 2011, private companies were already hard at work designing and testing reusable rockets. The companies hoped to take over sending astronauts and supplies to the ISS.

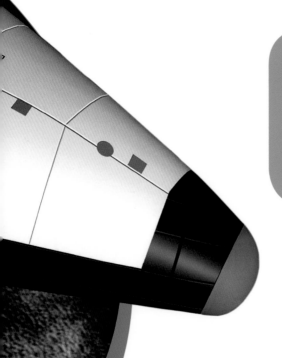

THINK ABOUT IT

Why do you think NASA canceled the space shuttle program if astronauts still needed to travel to and from the ISS?

The bell-shaped *Dragon* capsule holds passengers on board the Falcon 9 rocket.

Chapter 4

Grasshopper and Falcon

A company called SpaceX began building a reusable rocket in 2002. The rocket was known as the Falcon 9. Its first stage had nine engines. A spacecraft called *Dragon* sat at the rocket's top. *Dragon* was designed to parachute into the ocean after its mission and be reused.

At first, each Falcon 9 rocket was used only once. However, after several successful flights, SpaceX was ready to try landing and recovering the first stage. This was a very difficult goal. To learn how to land the first stage, SpaceX built a rocket called Grasshopper. Grasshopper was a Falcon 9 first stage with only one engine. It had four legs for landing. Grasshopper never went to space. However, SpaceX engineers used it to conduct many tests.

The Falcon 9 Rocket

The Falcon 9 Rocket is approximately 230 feet high (70 meters) and weighs about 1.2 million pounds (550,000 kilograms).

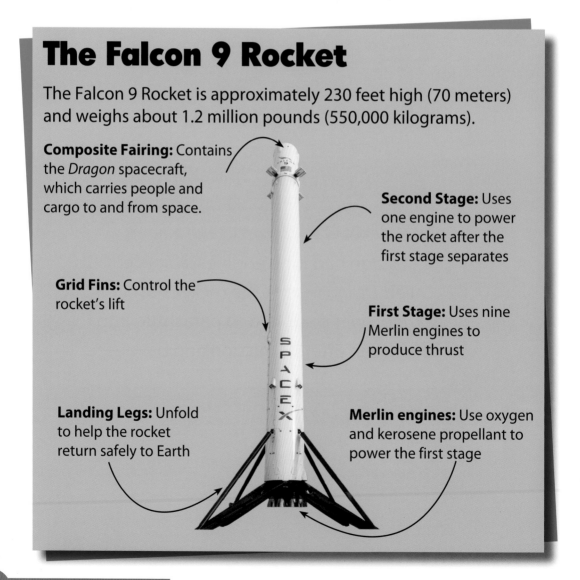

Composite Fairing: Contains the *Dragon* spacecraft, which carries people and cargo to and from space.

Second Stage: Uses one engine to power the rocket after the first stage separates

Grid Fins: Control the rocket's lift

First Stage: Uses nine Merlin engines to produce thrust

Landing Legs: Unfold to help the rocket return safely to Earth

Merlin engines: Use oxygen and kerosene propellant to power the first stage

Finally, they were ready to try landing a Falcon 9 first stage. Their first attempt took place in 2015. Minutes after launch, the first stage separated from the rocket. As the upper stages continued on toward space, the first stage fell back to Earth. Gas jets and small wings, or fins, helped steer the first stage toward a floating barge in the ocean. One minute before touchdown, the rocket's fin control system failed. The test ended in a crash.

However, engineers kept working. Later that year, a Falcon 9 first stage safely touched down on a landing pad at Cape Canaveral, Florida. It would soon be made ready for another flight. SpaceX was officially in the reusable rocket business.

Falcon 9 and the *Dragon* capsule were launched successfully on April 8, 2016 and returned safely without crashing.

Landing a Rocket

On May 1, 2017, SpaceX brought a Falcon 9 first stage safely back from outer space. Two minutes and 21 seconds after launch, the first stage's nine engines shut down. Next, the rocket stages separated. As the second stage headed into space, the first stage changed its direction by firing small nitrogen gas jets. Three of its engines fired to send it back toward the launch site. Then, more gas jets turned the first stage around so that its bottom pointed toward the ground. Another engine burn slowed the first stage's fall. To help keep the rocket aimed properly, four small fins opened near the rocket's upper end.

The engines shut down again, and the rocket gained speed as it neared the ground. Thirty seconds before landing, the rocket was falling at a speed of approximately 621 miles per hour (1,000 kilometers per hour). Next, the engines fired one last time. They slowed the rocket down to 0 miles per hour (0 km/h). Ten seconds from touchdown, four landing legs opened. Then, the rocket touched down on the landing pad.

The interior of the New Shepard capsule is capable of holding six people.

Chapter 5

Blue Origin

A company called Blue Origin is working on a reusable rocket, too. The rocket is called New Shepard. It is designed to be a fully reusable rocket. Unlike the SpaceX rockets, this rocket would carry tourists to outer space for a short time. The New Shepard rocket is 60 feet (18 m) tall. It has a bell-shaped capsule on top.

New Shepard has one liquid-fuel rocket engine at its base. Fins near the rocket's base can tilt to steer the rocket on a straight upward course.

New Shepard rockets have not been built yet. They are still being designed and tested. According to current plans, New Shepard would travel up to four times the speed of sound just seconds after launch. After slightly more than two minutes, the capsule would separate from the booster. The capsule's speed would cause it to continue to climb upward. As it climbed, passengers could float inside the capsule. They could enjoy great views out the windows until gravity caused the capsule to fall back down.

Meanwhile, the booster rocket would head back to the launch site. It would fire its engines a second time to decrease its speed. Fins and air brakes would also help slow its fall. The rocket would return to its launch pad. Four legs would open, and the rocket would touch down.

By this time, the capsule would have started falling back to Earth, too. Three parachutes would bring it back down. Small rockets on the capsule bottom would fire to cushion the landing.

Jeff Bezos is the founder of Blue Origin and Amazon, a multibillion-dollar online shopping and streaming company. On April 5, 2017, Bezos announced that he planned to spend $1 billion a year on his space venture.

New Shepard is not Blue Origin's only project in progress. The company is also designing a rocket known as New Glenn. It is named after John Glenn, the first U.S. astronaut to orbit Earth, in 1962. According to current plans, New Glenn will be a huge orbital rocket. It would be taller than the rockets built by SpaceX.

The first New Glenn rockets would have two stages. The first stage is designed to be reusable. It would land on a barge in the ocean. Then, it would be brought back to land for the next flight. Engineers are also planning a three-stage version. This rocket would be designed for heavy payloads. It would be taller than a 30-story building. It could potentially be used for missions to the Moon and to Mars.

On April 2, 2016, the New Shepard space capsule landed successfully in Van Horn, Texas.

Timeline

Designing reusable rockets has been very challenging. Despite numerous attempts, no fully reusable rocket systems have worked.

1950s Wernher von Braun designed a reusable rocket.

1981 The first space shuttle was launched. It was the first partially reusable rocket.

1996 X-33, the first reusable rocket, was designed by NASA.

2002 Elon Musk founded SpaceX. The company creates reusable rockets.

The International Space Station was completed. SpaceX will later launch reusable rockets and carry supplies to the ISS.

2011

2020 Russia plans to begin testing a reusable rocket.

Chapter 6

Multiple Methods

Not all companies plan to launch their rockets straight up. For example, a company called XCOR designed a small rocket plane that would take off from a runway and fly directly to space. This rocket plane, called Lynx, was designed to carry a pilot and one passenger who could conduct scientific experiments. However, Lynx would not go into orbit around Earth. Instead, it would return to Earth and land on a runway. However, the project was not a success. The company went out of business in 2017.

XCOR's Lynx was designed to fly more than 37 miles (60 km) above Earth's surface.

The Virgin Galactic *SpaceShipTwo* (SS2) was displayed at the Farnsworth Air Show in 2012.

Founded by Richard Branson in 2004, Virgin Galactic planned to develop commercial spacecraft for space tourism. The company has a two-part launch system. This system starts on an airport runway. It uses a carrier aircraft called WhiteKnightTwo to help launch its rocket. The carrier looks like two airplanes joined together wing to wing. It takes off from a runway. The *SpaceShipTwo* rocket is carried below WhiteKnightTwo's center wing.

At an **altitude** of 50,000 feet (15,240 m) above the ground, *SpaceShipTwo* is released. It fires its rocket engine and climbs to space. Because *SpaceShipTwo* starts out high above the ground, it does not need to use as much fuel to climb upward.

The *SpaceShipTwo* VSS Unity made its last powered test flight July 26, 2018. The company plans to test the vehicle once more in 2018. It could reach space in the near future and carry passengers not too long after that. Virgin Galactic hopes to build a fleet of spaceships over time.

The Sierra Nevada Corporation (SNC) is designing a reusable spacecraft that has short folding wings. The company plans to launch the spacecraft on top of a rocket, enclosed inside a shell. This shell is designed to open once the rocket reaches space. It would release a spacecraft called *Dream Chaser*. A pair of smaller rocket engines would propel the spacecraft to the ISS.

Scientists tested the *Dream Chaser* spacecraft at NASA's Dryden Flight Research Center in California.

Dream Chaser would have a disposable cargo module attached to its back end. This would allow it to transport cargo to space. Finally, with its wings unfolded, *Dream Chaser* would glide back to a runway on Earth. There, a crew would prepare it for another mission.

Dream Chaser can carry more than 12,000 pounds (55,000 kg) of **cargo** to space.

At the 34th Space Symposium in April 2018, SNC announced that *Dream Chaser* is scheduled to be launched in late 2020.

The **VSS Unity** is 60 feet (18 m) long and 27 feet (8 m) wide. Its **maximum speed** is 2,500 miles per hour (4,000 km/h).

Chapter 7

Space Tourism

Reusable rockets could provide cheaper ways to take cargo and astronauts to space. Soon, reusable rockets may make space flight possible for many people. For instance, Virgin Galactic's *SpaceShipTwo* is designed to carry two pilots and six space tourists. The rocket is not designed to go into orbit. Instead, it would land like an airplane at the end of the flight. Both parts could then be refueled and used again.

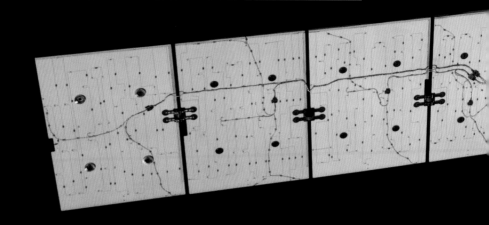

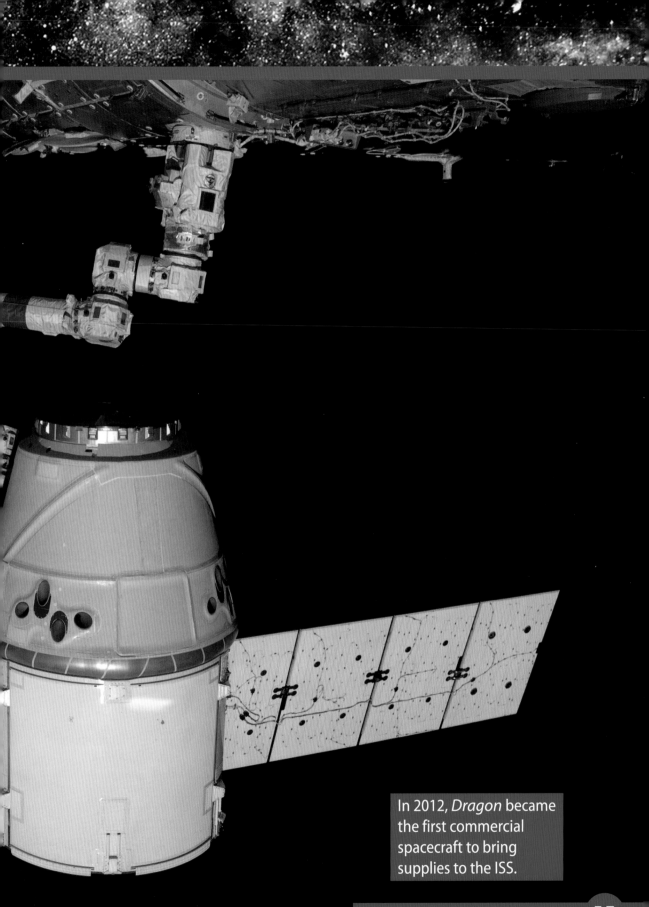

In 2012, *Dragon* became the first commercial spacecraft to bring supplies to the ISS.

SpaceX is also working on a flight for space tourists. A *Dragon* spacecraft would attach to the rocket. It would not have any SpaceX crew onboard. Instead, it would use an autopilot system. The rocket would take space tourists to the Moon.

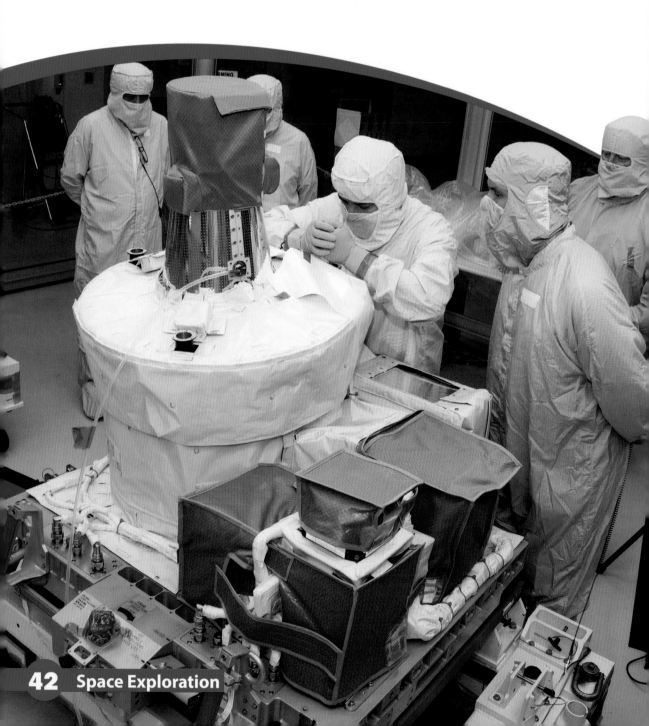

The trip would take about five days. The *Dragon* spacecraft would skim across the Moon's surface. However, it would not actually land. Instead, it would loop out beyond the Moon and return for one or more orbits. Finally, a rocket stage attached to the spacecraft would send the tourists back to Earth.

Reusable rockets are not yet common. However, scientists and engineers continue to work. In the future, reusable rockets may even carry tourists into outer space.

THINK ABOUT IT

What are the advantages of not having crew onboard? What are some disadvantages?

Scientists spend weeks and months preparing equipment for voyages, as they did in 2016.

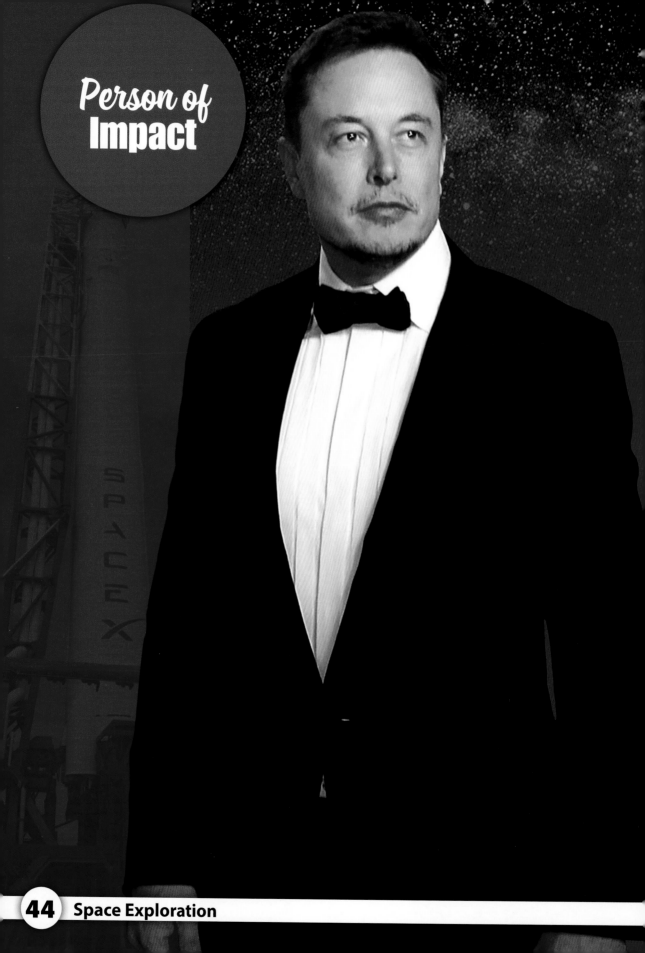

Person of Impact

Elon Musk

Elon Musk is the founder of SpaceX. Musk was born in South Africa in 1971. As a child, he was very interested in computers. He learned how to write computer programs. When he was 12 years old, he created and sold a computer game called *Blaster*.

Musk moved to Canada when he was 17 to attend Queen's University. Two years later, he transferred to the University of Pennsylvania. There, he studied physics and business. Musk then moved to Stanford University in California. Shortly afterward, he created an Internet company called Zip2.

Musk sold the company for many millions of dollars. He went on to form several other companies. His companies helped develop electric cars and solar power. One of his most exciting projects involves building reusable rockets. His rockets include the Falcon 9.

Musk's rockets are changing space transportation. Because the rockets can be used many times, they help reduce the cost of flying to space. However, Musk's vision goes beyond launching satellites, cargo, and people into orbit. His team is working on missions to the Moon. He even hopes to establish a colony on Mars.

Quiz

1 How many people can fit into the Blue Origin capsule?

2 What did the Saturn V do?

3 Who was Wernher von Braun?

4 What are the four forces in rocketry?

5 Why do engineers try to design rockets to be as light as possible?

6 What is the name of Elon Musk's space company?

7 What is the name of Virgin Galactic's latest *SpaceShipTwo* vehicle?

8 How many pounds of cargo can *Dream Chaser* carry?

Answers: 1. Six. **2.** It launched NASA astronauts to the Moon. **3.** NASA's leading engineer in the 1950s and 1960s. **4.** Lift, drag, gravity, thrust. **5.** Heavier rockets need more force and propellants to move. **6.** SpaceX. **7.** VSS Unity. **8.** 12,000.

Key Words

altitude: height above the ground

atmosphere: the layers of gases that surround a planet or moon

booster: the first stage of a large rocket, or a small rocket added to the side of a large rocket for extra thrust

capsule: the section of a spacecraft that carries the crew and often returns to Earth by parachute

friction: a force generated by the rubbing of one thing against another

orbit: to repeatedly follow a curved path around another object because of gravity

payload: an object carried to space by a rocket or other vehicle

propellants: a combination of fuel and oxygen that burns in a rocket engine to create thrust

satellites: objects or vehicles that orbit a planet or moon, often to collect information

stages: segments of a larger rocket that drop off after using all of their fuel

Index

Log on to www.av2books.com

AV² by Weigl brings you media enhanced books that support active learning. Go to www.av2books.com, and enter the special code found on page 2 of this book. You will gain access to enriched and enhanced content that supplements and complements this book. Content includes video, audio, weblinks, quizzes, a slideshow, and activities.

AV² Online Navigation

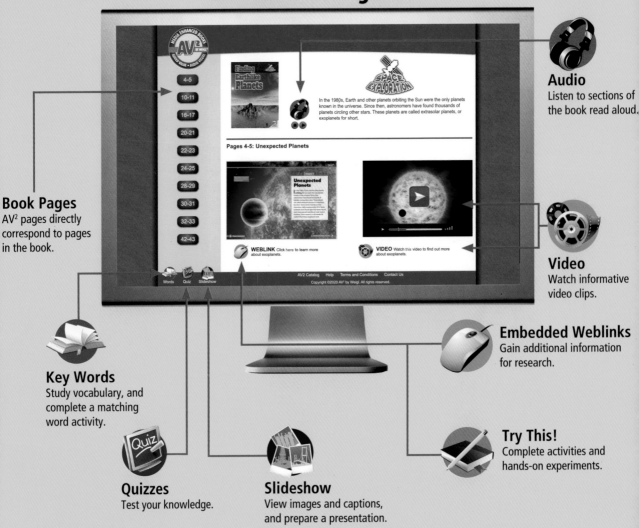

Audio
Listen to sections of the book read aloud.

Book Pages
AV² pages directly correspond to pages in the book.

Video
Watch informative video clips.

Embedded Weblinks
Gain additional information for research.

Key Words
Study vocabulary, and complete a matching word activity.

Try This!
Complete activities and hands-on experiments.

Quizzes
Test your knowledge.

Slideshow
View images and captions, and prepare a presentation.

AV² was built to bridge the gap between print and digital. We encourage you to tell us what you like and what you want to see in the future.

Sign up to be an AV² Ambassador at www.av2books.com/ambassador.